Be Your Own "Real Life" Superhero

Core Values That Empower Everyday People to Be Extraordinary in Life & Work

Sam Glenn

Award Winning Motivational Superhero

www.SamGlenn.com

"I believe there is a hero in all of us that keeps us honest, gives us strength, and makes us noble..."

- Aunt May, Spiderman 2

To be inspired is great, but to be an inspiration is an honor. When you are living a positive life, you will inspire others to live positive.

Why I Wrote This Book

One day, my daughters were climbing over everything in my office (myself included). I was trying to clean the office, but my little girls made it their mission to distract me and undo my hard work. They eventually noticed a Batman mask sitting on the corner of my desk, which I found after cleaning up holiday boxes. I forgot about it until my girls, who are ages two and three at the time of this writing, asked me to try it on, which I did. I figured they would both be scared by the mask. On the contrary, they thought it was the coolest thing ever. They laughed, giggled, and jumped around in excitement because they also wanted to wear the mask.

My oldest daughter asked, "Daddy, are you the real Batman?"

I looked at her, and replied with my best Batman impersonation, "I am the real Batman!" Again, both of them laughed, and we had fun with it. (I might add that the dogs do not like when I become Batman. They bark up a storm.)

After I was finally able to clean my desk, I glanced over at the Batman mask, and then a thought struck me. Perhaps it was an epiphany - a sudden, intuitive perception of or insight into the reality or essential meaning of something, usually initiated by some simple, homely, or commonplace occurrence or experience. Looking at the Batman mask, I felt a sense of meaning; a mission for myself and a message which I could share to inspire others.

The epiphany made me realize that I want my daughters to see me as one of their greatest superheroes. I want to be a superhero to my wife. I want to be a superhero to the audiences who listen to my speeches. I felt that spark of enthusiasm that happens when you connect to your purpose. I noticed something immediately. When I started to think of myself as a real life superhero, I started to think and act differently. No, I didn't use the blanket on our bed as a cape or try to melt steel with lasers from my eyes. Rather, I started to look for ways to become a better dad, husband, and professional speaker. My efforts and attitude transcended to a new level. It was evident that my inner superhero was showing up, and the impact was very real.

What does a superhero look like in real life? To be perceived as a real life superhero, I recognized that I needed to live, think, and make choices like a superhero. When you view yourself as a superhero, your thoughts and actions change. You are fueled by a purpose! The superheroes of our world take beneficial actions and make confident choices that result in rewarding outcomes for other people and themselves.

While becoming a real life superhero may sound alluring, let me be clear: your life will not necessarily get easier afterwards. It will, however, enable you to evolve into a better person, as well as become more resilient and give the best you've got.

My message is simple: we all can be our own unique, real life superheroes. That is a mouthful, but it's true. The following pages will help you unleash your superpowers for the good of mankind.

community, state, country, and possibly the whole world. There is no limit on where your difference will leave its impact. It doesn't matter what your vocation is, what industry you work in, or what role or title you have; you can be a real life superhero wherever you are.

As there is only one Superman or one Wonder Woman, there is now, and will only ever be, one of you. You are your own unique superhero. Your goal is to be the best real life superhero you can be. I want to challenge you to start looking for opportunities to demonstrate your unique greatness in your professional and personal life.

How Well Do You Know and Use Your Real Life Superpowers?

Before we dive into the meat and potatoes of this book, I want to start with a short exercise that will help bring clarity to what exactly your superpowers are.

So, grab a pen or pencil. (You will need it.)

Step 1: Identify Your Three (3) Greatest Strengths in Life

Write them in below. If you want to list more, you can. There are also additional blank pages in the back of this book for notes.

My greatest strengths in life are:

1.
2.
3.

These strengths are your unique "superpowers."

Here are mine, for reference:

Sam's Greatest Superpowers:

1. Sense of humor.
2. Leadership.
3. Creativity.

Step 2: Every Superhero Needs a Theme Song

You gotta have some tunes! It may sound slightly cheesy, but you would do well with a tune or tunes that can hype you up, raise your level of energy and wake up your spirit with enthusiasm. What's your superhero theme song? It must excite you, energize you, and compel you to step up. It shouldn't be a sad, soulful, or slow song that conjures negative emotions. It should ROCK! Find some tunes that make you want to MOVE! If you have more than one, list them all, and call it your playlist.

My superhero theme song(s) is/are:

1.
2.
3.

Here are my theme songs, for reference:

1. "Thunderstruck" by AC/DC.
2. "Immigrant Song" by Led Zeppelin.
3. "Anything" by U2.
4. Any song by The Spice Girls. (Just kidding! Or am I...?)

(Our superhero theme songs may change over time, and that's okay! Add them to your greatest superhero collection.)

A little side note: I think it is also a good idea to have music set aside to decompress you at the end of a stressful day (or week!). This music should relax you and allow you to de-stress. An overabundance of stress may act as the "Kryptonite" of our superpowers. As I am writing this book, I am listening to the soundtrack to Rudy. I go on YouTube, find relaxing playlists, and save them. I encourage you to do the same if you need a creative way to unwind, calm your mind, and let go of all the stress from the day. Music sure helps in many ways.

Hardships often prepare ordinary people for an extraordinary destiny

C.S. Lewis

One day, you will be just a memory for some people. Do your best to be a good one.

Real Life Superheroes:
Get a Little Better Everyday

Pablo Casals, the great cellist, was asked why, at eighty-five years old, he continued to practice five hours a day. He replied, "Because I think I'm getting better."

A friend, who manages a successful company, shared with me his philosophy on why he buys everyone books and promotes personal improvement in the workplace.

"Sam, I want my employees to work harder on themselves than they do on their job. When they get better at who they are, they become awesome at what they do. That is what we want, that is what we have, and that is why we are a success!"

I heard this quote once, and it has stayed with me since: "When we get better, it becomes a gift to others."

If you know my history, you know that I accidentally knocked over the legendary Zig Ziglar at a buffet we both attended. It was well over twenty years ago, and I had no idea who he was at the time. If you have never heard of Zig – he is a legend. Google him, and check out some of his videos. He is someone who really inspires and knows how to motivate.

For the record, I am not a buffet bully, but if I remember correctly, I was reaching for the bacon, and Zig was bouncing off my chest. We got to talking a little bit, and he introduced me to his wife, Jean Ziglar, who he fondly called The Red Head.

Zig was a very humble guy and very generous with his time. He became a friend and a mentor. More than anything, he encouraged me to get a little better every day. In one of our early morning conversations, he mentioned that he would read up to three hours every day. He said he did that because the input from reading became evident in the output in his life – his relationships, health, work, etc.

I wasn't a big reader at the time, but I started small by reading one page of a good book every day. Soon, it became two pages a day, and slowly evolved. The idea was to get a little better every day.

you are destined to repeat those mistakes. Learn and apply the wisdom of your own past experiences.

Never stop getting a little bit better every day. Read something new, learn something new, do something new. Remember, you don't have to be perfect, but choose to improve YOU and your life a little bit every day. When you do this, you not only become a superhero to others, you become a superhero to yourself.

Never trust your fears. Lean on your strengths!

You are what you are and you are where you are because of what has gone into your mind. You change what you are and you change where you are by changing what goes into your mind.

The Legendary Zig Ziglar

Real Life Superheroes:
Do the Little Things, But with a Big Heart

Can you think of a time when you did something that really didn't seem like a big deal to you, but to someone else it was HUGE DEAL? You made their day!? You see, being a real life superhero isn't about doing the big things. Rather, it's doing the little things with a big heart and a superhero's attitude. That is powerful. For example, my wife was getting our girls ready for a play date and she was running behind. I had been in my office working on a project, and I was in the zone. Meaning, I was totally focused, engaged, and getting stuff done. However, I paused from working for a few minutes to make some snacks for the girls to take with them, get their shoes on, and help put them in the car. I didn't think it was a big deal at all. However, my wife sent me a text message later, praising me for helping her get the girls ready and out the door. To her, it was a huge deal. I was the hero! Now, I wasn't trying to score points with my wife or anything like that. I was just doing what was right: jumping in, lending a helping

Having a soft heart in a cruel world is courage, not weakness.

Katherine Henson

If you cannot
do great things,
do small things
in a great way.

Napoleon Hill

Real Life Superheroes:

Learn, Live, and Pass on the Lessons from Their Own Personal Superheroes

Can you think of someone who was a superhero to you at some point in your life? When I think of my personal superheroes, it fills me with an overwhelming sense of gratitude. My superheroes have given, and continue to offer, valuable lessons that I can learn from and apply to my own set of life circumstances.

If you can reflect on the superheroes in your past and present, take time to acknowledge the lessons they taught and continue to teach you. The lessons granted to us by our personal superheroes are gifts that equip us with strength, empathy, wisdom, and inspiration. We honor our superheroes by applying the examples they set for us. We pay it forward by doing for others what our real life superheroes did for us.

Recently, I posted a question on my Facebook fan page **(samglennspeaks)** asking what others thought it meant to be a real life superhero. I got this amazing response...I had to add it to this book.

"A superhero in my eyes is someone that gives of oneself, especially when there's a sacrifice." She said, "My mom has always been a kind of superhero to me. When I was little, my mom would do thoughtful and time-consuming things for me, like painting clear jelly shoes with red glittery nail polish so I could have ruby slippers like Dorothy. As an adult, my mom has been a support in the most difficult times. Once, my infant daughter was sent to the ER for a medical concern. Without being asked, my mom arrived unexpectedly. She had been spending numerous hours a day already at another hospital with my dad, who was in the ICU. She was already stressed and exhausted. And there she was, comforting her granddaughter and singing 'Twinkle, Twinkle, Little Star' as a few nurses struggled to administer her IV. My mom was there comforting me, as well. I have no idea where she found the strength and emotional resources to still give of herself. The only explanation I have is that she's a mom. She is my real life superhero."

Real life superheroes are
superbly reliable,
authentically relentless
and exceptionally resilient!

Real Life Superheroes:

Become Super Positive by Becoming Super Grateful

The other day, I was having a rough day. ROUGH! It just seemed like everything was going wrong. It was one thing after another. It was like I was on a museum tour of Murphy's Law. Murphy's Law says that anything that can go wrong, will go wrong. That pretty much summed up my day.

On days like this, I noticed my mind gravitates toward what is not great in my world. The negative mind attracts more negativity. It makes you feel down, defeated, and sometimes depressed. You start to complain about little things, and if you are really having a bad day, you may start going back into your past and complaining about stuff that is done and over. Have you ever done that? You begin to replay every bad moment in your life, and then the pity party begins.

I was on my way home after an eventful day, and I was sitting in the airport coffee shop enjoying a pumpkin spice latte. I thought sitting down for a few minutes might help me get my bearings on the day. For years, I have been telling leaders and audiences that the fastest way to a better attitude – a more positive attitude – starts with thinking about what you are most grateful for. When you think of what you are most happy about or grateful for in your life, your attitude shifts directions, and you begin to have clearer and healthier thoughts. One thing I have learned is that our minor negatives have no chance of survival in the presence of our major positives.

In that moment, did I really feel like thinking about what I was most grateful for? NO. The feeling to do the work wasn't there. That is the part we must overcome. Our feelings can hold us back if we allow them to. I kind of wanted to drink my coffee and have a pity party. But, my wife sent me a video of our girls playing, and I started to think about how grateful I was for them. I felt a small shift in my mind. I started to think about what I was grateful for in the day. And then it happened. A few tables away, a woman sat down to enjoy a cup of coffee with her friend. She looked happy, like there wasn't a problem in the world. She seemed to have the attitude that said, "Life may not be perfect, but I am going to find the best I can in this day."

Her friend was kind enough to lift up a cup of coffee so she could have a sip. You see, this woman had no arms, yet she was happy in the moment. And then I realized, as I lifted my cup of coffee to take a sip, that I have absolutely nothing to complain about on this day. This stranger with no arms spoke to me through her attitude and actions. Maybe her life isn't always easy, but maybe she makes her life a little better by embracing and remembering all she has to be grateful for in the moment.

Real life superheroes become more positive as they become more grateful. The moment you start to feel sorry for yourself, think about what you love, what makes you happy, and what you are most grateful for. When you do this, you will notice a shift in your mind – a shift of strength and positivity will begin to take over, and empower you to bounce back, end the pity party, and celebrate the gift of who you are and what you have.

How you treat people says everything about you and the organization you represent

Real Life Superheroes:
Are a Source of Motivation, Inspiration, and, Sometimes, Tough Love

Sometimes, we need to be pushed to reach our true potential. I know I do! We need superheroes who will be honest and direct with us; who will tell it like it is; who will voice their apprehensions truthfully and lovingly. I would not be speaking professionally today without the superheroes in my life who did precisely those things.

I will admit that there have been times where I have been my own biggest limitation. Meaning, I get in my own way to block the success I desire. In those tough times, it was my real life superheroes that helped me stay on the right course of action and keep the right attitude. These types of superheroes may be coaches, mentors, friends, and family. They are people who we trust and who we know have our best interests at heart and in mind. They may share something with you that stings at first, but if you know they care about you, and you trust them, you know they are saying it for the betterment of your life. Before you react or make negative assumptions, listen, take in their advice or encouragement, and let it simmer inside your mind and heart a little. Are they trying to help you get better, be better, and live better? There have been moments, when I have received that dose of tough love that doesn't sound super great at first, but the message helped change my life, and made me a better person.

When I think of superheroes giving a little motivation and tough love, I absolutely think of this excerpt from the movie Rocky (below). Sometimes, we need the fire of motivation to push us to get up, keep going, and get better.

"You can either watch it happen or make it happen."

Elon Musk

Real Life Superheroes:
Greatest Superpower is Their "ATTITUDE"

Real life superheroes believe that their greatest superpower is their ATTITUDE. The concept of using your attitude as a superpower works like this: if you choose the right attitude, it will work for you and create positive consequences. If you choose a poor attitude, it will frustrate you and create negative consequences. Keep in mind, having a positive attitude doesn't stop adversity or negative things from happening in life. However, having the right attitude equips you with the mental stamina, clarity, creativity, and resilience to deal with whatever life throws your way. Learn from it, grow from it, become strengthened by it, and keep moving forward. That is the power of having the right attitude working for you. That is an incredible superpower! Your attitude can, and will always be, one of your greatest superpowers if you learn to use it right.

The key is, you must practice getting, keeping, and implementing the right attitude. What empowers an attitude to be "right" or "positive" is feeding your attitude positive, inspiring, and educational material. I suggest reading good books. Listen to inspiring audio recordings. Be around people who bring out your best. Make choices that make you feel good about yourself and life. Eliminate bad habits, bad company, and establish boundaries with those who try to weaken your attitude.

It is also pertinent that you develop a deeper awareness of how your attitude is functioning through your work, communication, how you treat others, how you handle challenges, how you treat yourself, and how you manage your thinking process – the way you handle pressure, adversity, and conflict. A deeper attitude awareness will help you understand how your attitude is functioning in your life, and what adjustments you may need to make it work better for you. If your attitude is not working in your favor in a certain area of your life, then it's simple; you need to make some adjustments. There is nothing bad about that; it's just part of the process and maintenance of developing a superhero attitude. You can't wish for a better attitude, you must work to create it.

Remember, your attitude is always at work. It works only the way you decide to make it work. The process of getting, keeping and applying the right attitude takes some effort on your part. Evaluate your attitude and give yourself a performance review - what is great about your attitude? What needs to change? What can you do to take it to a new level? How is your attitude affecting your relationships? How do others perceive your attitude in the workplace? How do you deal with others who are negative? Is your attitude a good example? Would your favorite sports team be inspired to win with your present attitude? Would people line up to work next to you because of your attitude, or would they choose a different option? Think about it.

If you want to take another route, invite someone you look up to and trust - a mentor or a coach - who can help you evaluate the state of your attitude and how it is working in your life.

Take a few moments, and reflect on the role your attitude is playing in the significant areas of your life. If you want, jot down any thoughts about this in the back of this book.

Spend a little time and work on developing a better attitude because it will only help you become a better real life superhero. We will discuss some simple ways you can do this in the following pages.

there is something inside me that finds delight in doing complimentary customer service training for employees for this company.

(This retail giant was once invigorated by a spirit of integrity, service, leadership, excellence, and enthusiasm. They cared, and that got people excited about shopping and working there. Sadly, that has all moved into a questionable hibernation.)

After the manager had aggressively snapped at me for absolutely no reason, I thought for a moment that maybe she was having a bad day, and I just got stuck in the path of her storm. Maybe her position was under a lot of pressure. Maybe someone called in sick, and she was scrambling to fill the shift. Maybe her car wasn't running right, or her kids left their smelly shoes in there, and it smells badly. Maybe she didn't feel good. These were some possible things that were putting a limp in her attitude. So, I decided the best thing to do – the right thing to do – was to share my attitude with her. I leaned forward, smiled, and playfully said, "I would like to buy you a Snickers bar."

She paused, turned to me with a curious smile, and said, "Pardon me?"

I said, "I would like to buy you a Snickers bar because when you're having a bad day, you are not quite yourself."

She started laughing like what I said made her day, and I think it did. I was just imitating the recent Snickers commercial. She stopped what she was doing and said, "Follow me, I will take care of you."

She made me what I, the customer, wanted to be – a priority! That is what every customer wants and deserves. She changed the battery in my watch with a smile. I made her day, and she ended up making mine. She didn't start out strong, but she changed her attitude, and finished strong. That is huge! Attitude changes everything!

I thought about giving her a copy of one of my books to say thank you for helping me the way she did, but her company has a very strict policy that doesn't allow their employees to accept any inspirational or motivational gifts. Employees can actually lose their job if they accept such a gift even though it could improve their service abilities, make their workplace better, or help them learn new leadership skills. I would hate to see someone lose their job over something like that. That would just be horrible!

Even at your best, someone will have something negative to say. The solution is to just keep doing your best and giving your best anyway. Let the evidence of your attitude and actions silence your critics.

Real Life Superheroes: Use These Essential ACTIONS to Keep a Healthy and Super Positive Attitude

Your attitude is either in the way or making a way, and you determine which – every day. It is having the presence of mind to know if your attitude is working for you or against you. Here are some very simple actions you can take to keep a healthy and super positive attitude.

1. A positive attitude doesn't stop adversity from happening, but what it does do is give you the mental clarity, creativity, and calmness to align yourself to deal better with life's challenges. A negative attitude in the face of adversity will defeat your best efforts. Think for a moment of some ways you can respond when life gives you upsetting challenges. These are your preplanned actions so you don't do something destructive or act in a way that is harmful. For example, when I feel really stressed, I like to go for a long walk. If it's late at night, I like to watch a funny movie or

paint in my studio. Identify what works best for you, so when there is a bump in your day, you can implement what calms you down and keeps the right mental perspective.

2. Nobody can choose your attitude but you. You are the owner of your attitude, not anyone else. Remember this the next time someone tries to push your bad day buttons. They have no power over your attitude.
3. Every time you subtract negative from your life, you make room for more positive. Is there a habit or person that really fills your life with toxic energy and outcomes? It may be time to make some changes that no longer involve what brings out your worst. Your goal is to be around people and do activities that bring out your best. Sometimes you have to let things go. You can choose to let it define you, confine you, refine you, outshine you, or you can choose to move on and leave it behind you.
4. Input creates output. What you read, listen to, and who you associate with is input, and it eventually leads to your output - your attitude, effort, and

choices. You are reading this book, but go to the bookstore and look for other books you can fill your mind with. This is my #1 go to tool for creating, empowering and employing the right attitude in my life. I am always working to make it better and make it work for me.

5. Your attitude doesn't have to be perfect; however, be willing to EDIT your thinking, delete the kind of thinking that isn't good for you, and accept new thinking that is positive for you. Do you replay negative thoughts from your past or just think the worst all the time? Hit your edit button, and get rid of that junk. Practice new, dominating thoughts that overpower the worry, fear, and doubtful thinking that may creep up and try to live rent free in your mind. I like the saying, "Nobody with dirty feet can live in my mind rent free! They are gone! Outta here! See ya!"
6. Things will go wrong and challenge our attitude. It is easy to get negative. It is okay to get mad about something, but don't let your anger determine your behavior or push you to make a bad choice that you will regret. When life gives

you a situation that upsets you, you always have a choice to make it better or worse. You can react or respond. Step back, think, examine your options, and get your mind right before you do or say anything.

7. A positive quote a day helps keep a negative attitude away. A positive quote is an attitude vitamin. It takes about thirty seconds to read an uplifting quote, and it feeds your attitude the positive nutrition it needs to be positive. Get a quote book, and read it daily.
8. The fastest way to transform your attitude from negative to positive is to identify what you are most grateful for. This is magical. Your minor negatives have no power in the presence of your major positives. Think about your family, what you love, and everything you have to be grateful for. This is so powerful.
9. To fill your attitude with hope, purpose and meaning, you have to have a positive expectation for your life – something to look forward to. It can be a dream, a goal, or something small and simple to look forward to. Some also call it, "Dream big

dreams!" Have a goal, a dream or something to work towards that gets you excited, and challenges you to experience life beyond the walls of your comfort zone. Plan little things to look forward to. It can be a trip to recharge your batteries. It can be an adventure. A new business start-up. Visit an old friend, and reconnect. Having something to look forward to gives us hope, meaning, and purpose. Try it, it works!

10. The way we communicate determines responses in others. If you treat others negatively, you can expect others to respond much the same way. If you treat others with a positive attitude, a majority of the responses will be positive. Think before you communicate. For example, if you want others to treat you better, start by treating others better. This doesn't mean that some people won't treat you poorly, but it means more people will start treating you better. Communication is a powerful thing.

11. Your greatest distraction in life is a negative thought. The more you entertain it by thinking about it and believing in it, the bigger the thought

becomes, and the greater the harm it will have on you. Distract or interrupt your mind with a different thought. I mentioned this a little earlier, but you control your thinking. A way to push out these negative thoughts is by reading positive material, doing positive activities, and creating boundaries from people and situations that bring out your worst.

12. If a positive attitude can make life better and business better, then why doesn't everyone get one? The answer is either they don't care, don't get it, or have a minimal appraisal of how valuable attitude is. Your attitude will improve and be more powerful when you become the kind of person who cares. The more you care, the more you will make having the right attitude a priority.

Life doesn’t give us purpose, we give life purpose.

The Flash

"I have no idea where I am going to be tomorrow. But, I accept the fact that tomorrow will come and I'm going to rise to meet it."

Wonder Woman

Real Life Superheroes: Are on a Mission Fueled by Purpose and Enthusiasm

I love the example of two guys mopping floors at NASA headquarters, and they were both asked how their day was going. The first guy responded, "New day, same old stuff."

The second guy responded with enthusiasm, "Today is outstanding, and we are sending people into space!"

One guy didn't see a mission in what he was doing, while the other guy connected his role as an important part of the big picture. It provided him with more purpose in his daily work. Therefore, it was probably reflected in how he did his work and the results he created. When purpose is involved in our work, it's revealed with authority.

A few years ago, I was in the market for a new truck, so I went, on the recommendation of a friend, to explore my buying options at a particular dealership. He was right; the experience was different than what I expected. I had the chance to speak a little with the owner of the dealership, and he said to me, "Sam, we are not here to sell you a car. Anyone can do that, but we are not anyone. We are here to serve and provide all your transportation needs for you and your family for the rest of your life, and we hope you live a long time."

Real life superheroes have a handle on what is driving their ship - meaning their life and organizational success. Simon Sinek calls it, "Connecting to your WHY."

When you understand your "WHY" - why you do what you do - something happens. You feel a greater sense of purpose and enthusiasm mustering up in your soul and mind. You no longer go through the motions to get something done; you do what you have to do with a greater sense of meaning, contribution, excellence, and impact. Sometimes, to rekindle our purpose in life and generate a spark of enthusiasm, we need to evaluate why we do what we do. Do you have a job, work just to get a paycheck every week, or is it something more like providing for your family and saving for the future? It's the same income, but all are different purposes. One lacks purpose, and the other fuels you with it.

Real life superheroes take and make the time to evaluate why they do what they do often to ensure their purpose is staying on track and there is fuel in the tank to do what has to be done. When you operate from a place of purpose, you are going be excited about the work you do, and that transfers to the people you serve, as well.

Our value doesn't decrease based on someone's inability to see your worth.

Real Life Superheroes: Use Enthusiasm to Transform the Ordinary into the Extraordinary!

The other day, I was walking through the airport to my gate and something caught my attention – it was enthusiasm in action! There was a crowd of people gathering around a piano player. You could hear cheers and people clapping. The energy of what was going on grabbed my attention and pulled me in. It turns out it was a young man on a piano, playing songs we all knew and loved. Some were older tunes, some were new; however, it was evident he wasn't just playing the songs to play the songs. He was putting something behind that music that brought it to life. He played with such excitement and passion that you not only heard the music, you felt it in your soul. I actually got goose bumps. His enthusiasm was contagious, so much so that people took a detour from their scheduled plans just to watch him play for a few minutes. The crowd smiled, cheered, laughed, clapped, opened up their wallets, and gave him generous tips. It was impressive. This piano player took ordinary songs and transformed them into an extraordinary experience. We can learn from him by applying this to our own lives. If we just settle for going through the motions of what we do daily, we become like zombies. But, if we put a little heart into what we do, it comes to life or, as I like to say – magic happens!

Don't be a zombie. Zombies have no enthusiasm. NONE! The music is a metaphor. You can either just play the music or you can give the music life with your enthusiasm.

Do what you are expected to do, and you survive. Do more than you are expected to do, and you will thrive.

It’s not who I am underneath, but what I do that defines me.

Batman

Real Life Superheroes:
Believe in the Greatness of Who They Are, What They Can Do, and Who They Can Become

One thing I enjoy is following artists on Instagram. I love painting, and I appreciate the talent of other artists. I like to see their works develop. It's my passion. My big dream is to create art full-time one day. I want to use my art to raise money for special causes. It will eventually happen. I believe it will.

One day, as I was browsing artists online, I noticed one particular artist who is very talented, but filled with self-defeating doubt. He was posting pictures of his art at a flea market and remarking how nobody was buying his stuff. As the day progressed, he kept discounting his art. By the end of the day, the paintings were selling for less than the cost of materials, and even then, his art did not sell. He posted his thoughts about quitting, and that his dream of being a full-time artist was just a waste of time. His rants were negative and self-defeating. In fact, many people commented that he should give up and get a job, and that some dreams are not meant to come true.

I couldn't take it anymore. I had to reach out and share some encouragement. I informed him that he needs to start valuing his art more. If he doesn't value it, nobody else will. I could tell he doubted himself, and, as a result, he doubted his art. His art is amazing, and his doubt is such a disservice to his God-given talents and finished artwork.

I gave him a few ideas on how he could turn things around and help people discover more meaning and value in his work. One key point I reinforced was that he absolutely needed to start believing in himself. I encouraged him to stop posting so many negative comments about himself and his art. Instead of allowing people to experience his greatness, he was putting out sample trays of his toxic thinking. His attitude was his biggest roadblock to success, and he was feeding that limitation every day with more and more doubt. So, I shared this little poem with him because whenever I begin to doubt my greatness or purpose in this world, I read this poem, and it reminds me that I have absolutely no reason to doubt my value in the world. You need to believe this for yourself, as well. When you believe in yourself, miracles happen, doors open, and opportunities come knocking.

You are much stronger
than you think you are.
Trust me.

Superman

“We choose what holds us back and what moves us forward.”

Master Splinter, Teenage Mutant Ninja Turtles

"Just because someone stumbles and loses their way, it doesn't mean they are lost forever."

Charles Xavier, X-Men

A mistake that makes you humble is better than an achievement that makes you arrogant.

Real Life Superheroes: Use GOOD HUMOR to Eliminate Stress and Negativity

I was having a conversation the other day with a friend who is in his 80s, and I asked him if he could do one thing over in life, what would it be? His response was simple and straight to the point: "Sam, I would relax more, lighten up, and not take everything so seriously."

That's great advice. We need not get so worked up about the little things. Wouldn't you agree?

So, how do you accomplish this? Through conscious choice and practice. Next time something starts making your blood boil; step back, breathe, and find a healthy distraction that changes your focus. One thing that relaxes me is trying to look for the lighter side in situations. A few years ago, I lost a small bag at the airport. It was about the size of a shaving kit bag, so it wasn't that big. I used it to put all my valuables in one place. It had all my cash, my iPod, my watch, and, believe it or not, a coupon to Arby's fast food restaurant. How that coupon got into my little bag, I will never know.

As soon as I realized I couldn't find my bag, I began to panic. If you have ever lost your keys or something of value, you know the feeling. I looked all over for the bag. I felt my stomach doing flips because I couldn't find it. I was so frustrated. Finally, I went to the security office to report the missing bag or see if someone turned it in. However, I knew in the back of my mind that nobody would turn it in. It was long gone. Let's be real, it was a gift bag to anyone who found it. When I explained all this to my wife over the phone, she encouraged me to relax and let it go. That was easier said than done, but I couldn't change the fact that it was gone, and I had made someone else's night.

So, I went to report my lost bag to the security, and as the security guy was taking notes, I began to take my wife's gentle advice and just relaxed. I took a few deep breaths and started informing the security personnel what items were in the lost bag. I said, "In the pouch were a few hundred dollars in cash, a beautiful watch, a brand-new iPod, and a coupon to Arby's." I continued to share my sentiments, "I don't really care about the money, watch, or iPod. However, I am deeply concerned about the Arby's coupon because it is set to expire soon."

The guy taking notes paused for a second, gave me a blank look, and then started laughing out loud. He got the humor. Using a little humor took the stress away and relaxed my nerves. The truth is that stuff like that is bound to happen at some point in our lives, and sometimes the best hand you can play is looking at the lighter side.

Not taking everything so seriously is choosing not to be worked up over something you have no control over. It could be a big deal, but choosing to relax about the situation will help you think better, calm your anxieties, and give your heart a calming break. I believe you get the picture. Relax! Lighten Up! Chill out! Don't take everything so seriously.

Real Life Superheroes:

Get Knocked Down, But They Bounce Back

Every now and then, we experience this unplanned event called a "bad day." They happen from time to time, and on those days, it seems like nothing goes right. A real life superhero recognizes that it normal to have those kinds of days, but not to wallow in them too long.

There are times in my own life when I thought, "I just need to stay home and not go out, answer the phone, or do anything." That's when you know you are having a really bad day.

Norman Vincent Peale once said, "The only people without problems are in a cemetery."

What does that mean? It means if you are alive, you are going to have potholes in your day. I remember being in high school, and my dad let me ride his brand-new, ten-speed bike around the block. He paid good money for that bike, and gave me a firm message before I took it out: "Sam, please be careful and don't ruin it."

I got halfway around the block, and something distracted me. Three seconds later, I was picking myself up off the road. My arms were scraped, and my knee was cut up. As I was getting my bearings, I saw that I had hit a giant pothole in the road. I looked over at the bike, and it was in worse shape than I was. My day just went from awesome to terrible!

I had to carry the bike home and tell my dad his new bike was ruined. The pothole destroyed it. The look on my dad's face made me think he wanted to make me look like the bike. I felt awful because I knew we didn't have a lot of money, and that was his way to exercise and get out to relax.

Some days, we get up thinking it's going to be a super awesome day. Then we show up to work, and someone is in a bad mood and snapping at you about everything. You know what I mean. You go from thinking, It's going to be a great day! to thinking, I might snap!

Things happen that interrupt our perfectly planned days. We have to deal with them the best we can, and move on. Easier said than done, I know, but superheroes do it.

My high school basketball coach used to tell me, "Sam, always be grateful for everything in your life, because someone, somewhere, has it a lot worse than you right now."

A bad day may distort your positive perspective of things, but work through it, bounce back, and move on. Don't turn a bad day into a bad week, month, or year. My new philosophy is that "Potholes happen!" Deal with them the best you can, bounce back, and move on.

Sometimes, you need to start your day over by saying, "The rest of my day will be the best of my day."

It never hurts to have a little pep talk with yourself to calm down, relax, think right, and respond to whatever circumstances going on in your life in a more proactive way. If you are reactive in your responses, you also need to be prepared to carry regrets. People who are reactive don't think about their responses, and will say or do things without clearly thinking it through. As a result, they pay a big price that can give a bad day a longer extension. The news is always filled with stories about road rage and situations where someone reacted, and will have to pay for it for a lifetime. Don't let that happen to you.

Next time you are having a bad day or just hit a pothole, stop what you are doing, have a cup of coffee, and just think for a bit. Calm your mind. Reflect on the best options for yourself. Think of a better way to manage your circumstance, and move on from it.

Maybe you need to take a short nap or go for a walk. A fifteen-minute walk can solve a lot more than two hours of worrying. Do something that distracts your mind from thinking in the wrong direction. Get over, around, under, and through your bad days with the force of clear and healthy choices.

Real Life Superheroes:

Might Save the Day, but Don't Always Get the Recognition They Deserve

A few years ago, I was at the St. Louis Airport waiting to board my flight. As I was sitting there, I noticed a little boy, about three or four years old, running around and burning off some energy. I saw his father observing him. As the kid was running carefree, there were these huge glass displays, and the little boy started running full speed towards one of them. He didn't see the glass. Just before impact, his dad swooped in, grabbed him, and pulled him up by the back of his jacket to avoid what could have been a very ugly accident. The little boy began crying because he thought his father was keeping him from having fun when, in reality, he just saved him from a world of pain.

Sometimes, real life superheroes put forth incredible effort in the dark hours when nobody is watching. They may arrive early to work or stay late. They might lend a helping hand when it's needed, but not required. They stretch themselves to do a little extra, but their extraordinary deeds often go unnoticed. It sounds a little uninspiring, but it makes you appreciate when you are appreciated. However, a real life superhero doesn't rely solely on recognition to do what is right. They are on a mission. They know who they are, and what they stand for. They keep doing what needs to be done until it gets done. They work on themselves to expand their educational platform. They understand when they learn new skills; they have more value to offer others.

Recognition does not determine how great a real life superhero will be. It doesn't influence their effort or attitude. Recognition or not, a real life superhero does whatever it takes.

Don't worry when you are not recognized, but strive to be worthy of recognition.

Abraham Lincoln

Real Life Superheroes:
Do the Right Things

It is so easy to cut corners and simply get by when it's convenient and nobody is looking. Real life superheroes adhere to the core value of doing the right things. They take ownership for their attitude and actions. They don't point the finger or play the blame game when things go wrong. They may be tempted to cut a corner, but they always summon the superpower of integrity, and do what is right. They live up to their word. If they say they will get back to you at 3:30 in the afternoon, they do it. They don't get back to you at 3:31 with an excuse. They do what they say they will do when they say they will do it.

When I was in college, my Dad's company hired me for a few weeks to load trucks for Wonder Bread. These bread racks were taller than me, and weighed a ton. They required you to move two at a time, but I could barely move one. One of the requirements for this job was to get steel-toe boots. They had a safety policy, to ensure everyone kept all their toes in case one of the big bread racks rolled over it. I was a college student, and I could not justify spending the extra money on new boots. I tried to cut the corner, and when you do the wrong things, there is always a consequence to pay.

I tried to be as careful as possible, but one evening, one of the bread racks rolled right over my foot. I was injured and ended up paying more than double the price for the boots because I had to go to the doctor and lost time at work. I lost more because I tried to cut corners and do things the wrong way. We always end up paying more when we do the wrong things. There are times when you might be in a rush, tired, or just don't feel like doing something correctly. In fact, you might debate in your mind about doing the right thing, the right way. Real life superheroes do not negotiate. They do what is right.

From an organizational standpoint, when people do the right things, the right way, they achieve the right results. And that is when you achieve recognition. That is what superheroes create when they do the right things. Attempting to get by doing what isn't right will always lead to a bigger and more expensive price to pay.

Real life superheroes do right by others by doing the right things the right way.

Superheroes do not live in their comfort zone.

Real Life Superheroes:
Lead by Example

Superhero Organizations Have One Distinct Quality in Common… They "CARE" About Their Superheroes!

I have had the privilege of working with some of the most amazing companies and outstanding leadership teams in the country. These organizations have made it a priority to create a workplace where people grow, have a purpose, and make a difference. They make it a priority to do something positive for their department, team, staff, associates, or the entire company. I am fortunate to have a job that allows me to be a part of so many of those special moments.

Sometimes, the groups I work with will do little things, and other times, they go big time. It all depends on the objectives of what they are trying to accomplish. Either way, they are investing in their people and making them feel recognized and valued. They take time to develop creative, fun, empowering, uplifting, and kind-hearted experiences for their people. I can say, without a doubt, never underestimate the incredible impact a group of caring and inspired people can make.

Creating an empowering workplace culture requires attention, consistency, investment, expectation, buy-in, and a caring heart. If a workplace is toxic, stale, or dull, it means the leadership is accountable for allowing it to get that way or letting it continue. They are responsible for that mess. The good news for you is that you can be in any role, at any level, have any title, work in any industry, and still have the power to improve the quality of your workplace culture. It all starts with your attitude! Superhero leaders don't wait for a green light to demonstrate leadership. They step up, do the right things, lend a helping hand, make things right, go above and beyond, fix what needs fixing, eliminates distractions, and makes great things happen.

Even if your workplace culture has positive momentum, I believe there are little things you can do to ensure it stays on track and keeps rising to new levels. Remember, everything follows our chosen and cultivated attitude.

It was nearly twenty years ago, when I had just started speaking professionally; I offered the leadership team at my mom's workplace a complimentary motivational presentation for their entire company. I pitched it to boost morale and alleviate some of the stress. It was a very stressful and highly demanding work environment. Also, looking back now, I think I just wanted to see my mom have a little happiness. The back story to this is that my mom's workplace was so negative and toxic that it often made her feel physically sick and unhappy. It was an organization that didn't care about their workforce. They just didn't. People didn't feel secure enough in their job and basically worked just hard enough not to lose their job. That was the extent of their employees' motivation – work hard enough not to get fired.

I am speaking from experience when I share this: when you have a family member who works in this kind of culture, it not only sucks the life out of the person you love, but it affects their families, as well. When your family member brings back that toxic workplace into the home, it's not healthy for anyone.

Not surprisingly, the leadership declined my offer, and they cited this reason: "It would be a distraction from staying focused on getting important work done."

Nowadays, not a week goes by that I don't get a few emails from people who say, "Sam, I wish you could come speak to our company; it is so negative around here. People are unhappy, and the morale is low."

I've heard it all! What I just shared is the abridged and sweet version of the emails people send me. I don't want to rob anyone of hope, but when people send me those types of emails, I immediately know the type of leadership, culture, and environment they work in. I have learned from experience spanning over twenty years that those kinds of leaders and companies would never hire a speaker like me. They don't see the value or purpose in it. They view it as an unnecessary expense instead of a necessary investment in growing and empowering their people in the direction of greatness. There is a huge difference. Even if I offered my services for free, these types of organizations and leaders would still think it would be a waste of time.

At this point, you might be thinking, Well, why don't they just leave that rotten job?

Some people wish they could, but they can't. They have a family that relies on them. They need the benefits. They have responsibilities tied to every penny in their paycheck. Do they want to leave? Probably every minute of the day, but they forge on and do the best they can. I try to do my part and encourage and inspire these people on a daily basis. If I can bring a little light into a part of their day, I know they will do better at their jobs and feel good about it. In situations like this, I often send a few free books or even shoot a short uplifting and funny video for their department to boost their spirits. Plus, I feel in my heart it's the right thing to do. I saw what that kind of work environment did to my mom, so I have a big heart for people who have to endure that type of culture day in and day out.

And please understand, I don't do things to be defiant towards the leaders of these types of organizations or try to rally a rebellion. That is not my role or who I am. I believe in respect, and it's not my place to share an opinion or be a source of conflict.

Offering a little encouragement to those who ask for it or giving away a few copies of my book is something I love to do, and it is the right thing to do. That's it! I work with superhero leaders every day in my job, and the one distinct quality superhero leaders and organizations have in common is they authentically care about their superheroes. They care about people at every level, in every office, every role, and every department. Everyone is cared for equally.

I recently spoke for Columbus Regional Health in Indiana, and one superhero employee shared this amazing story with me, "Sam, I went off and served in the war, and when I got back, I still had my job. When my house was flooded, they sent people from the hospital to help my family. I would never dream of leaving. I feel safe here. I feel like someone here."

And that, my friend, is a great picture of what caring for your superheroes is all about.

If you treat people like superheroes at work, they become superheroes in leadership, service, sales, teamwork, community, and life. If you want to see people rise, treat them like they can!

"If serving is beneath you, then leading is above you."

A. Brown

Being positive in a negative situation is not weakness. It's called leadership.

Real Life Superheroes:

Respect Others

Everyone is different. It's called diversity. Real life superheroes do not judge books by their cover. The world is a canvas filled with extraordinary art, but sometimes we get so focused on the messy things or judge the differences, that we truly miss the beauty that surrounds us. A real life superhero chooses to look for the good or beauty in others by offering respect, understanding, patience, listening, and encouragement.

I was about thirty minutes away from giving a speech on making positive choices to a gymnasium filled with high energy high school students. Before I was to speak, they had a talent show where students could display their special talents for all to see. As I waited backstage, I met a girl named Becky. She had wild green hair, and she had so many piercings, I jokingly thought she had fallen into a tackle box. We chatted a bit about all the earrings she had. I just wanted to know if they hurt. When I asked Becky how it was going to her school, her response was, "I hate it!"

"Why?"

"Because everyone makes fun of me for the way I look. Students are mean to me, and they don't even know me."

"That is too bad. I am sorry to hear that. You should never judge a book by its cover. So, what will your talent be today?"

"I am going to sing 'Amazing Grace.'"

"Well, good luck. I know you will do great!"

When it was Becky's turn to perform, the students got loud, and heckled her as she made her way to the microphone. They were rude and disrespectful. The principal had to walk out and reprimand them to quiet them down. I witnessed a book being judged by its cover. Becky waited for it to get as quiet as it would get, and began to belt out that wonderful melody of "Amazing Grace."

I have heard a lot of people sing "Amazing Grace," but I have never heard anyone sing it as well as Becky. I got goose bumps. Shocked by the captivating voice that filled the once-rowdy gymnasium, the students were silent and wide-eyed. When she finished, she received a standing ovation. Before I left the school that day, I overheard one of the students talking to Becky, and telling her how wonderfully she sang, but what really got my attention was learning that a young man apologized to Becky for being a bully and making fun of her.

We are all different, and have our own special uniqueness. You are an original. Nobody looks like you. If nobody has ever told you, let me be the first, "It is okay to be you."

Respect is treating others how you want to be treated. Nobody likes to be treated badly. Respecting others is acknowledging that we all are unique, and we don't all quite look the same, but we can get along.

I think life changed for Becky that day because people didn't see her as a green-haired girl who looked like she had fallen in a tackle box, but because people saw her for who she really was – a unique person. Before you judge that book by its cover, why not read the book a little, and get to know them and appreciate them for the gift of who they are?

Real life superheroes choose to respect and appreciate the special qualities and uniqueness in others. Instead of looking for every flaw in someone, they seek out the treasures. Instead of bringing someone down or judging them, they choose to understand, and offer respect and consideration.

Real Life Superheroes:

Change the World with Positive Actions, Not Good Intentions

The more you care, the more you will demonstrate it. The less you care, the less you will do. The amount we care shows up in how we treat others, treat ourselves, and do our work. There is always evidence that you care or you don't. Having good intentions doesn't get the job done. Taking positive action and actually doing something is what makes great things happen.

Remember, itis our actions that change the world, not our intentions. I was watching the Today Show, and they ran a story about a little boy who set up a lemonade-type stand at the end of his driveway with all his toys. He was giving his toys away to families in need, ones who couldn't afford toys for their kids. That little boy was already a big-time superhero. He didn't just care about something, he did something about it. He turned a good intention into a job well done.

Sometimes, after my speeches, I get people who come up and say, "I sure wish you could change this person's attitude and behavior."

I get what they are saying, but we can't change others. Our greatest leverage to change others' actions and attitudes is to be an example of the change we want to see. We can't just talk about it, we need to follow through and do it: we need to walk the talk.

Real life superheroes set an example for others to follow and replicate. Recently, I spent a few weeks in Texas, and flew out of Houston the day Hurricane Harvey hit. When I got home and saw what was happening on the news, I was in shock by the flooding and devastation.

What spoke volumes were the stories of people who sprang into action to help in the relief effort. People gave of their time, money, and resources to help. That was inspiring. It was action and not just good intentions that made the difference.

I love the one story the news ran about a Houston business man who selflessly opened up his two furniture stores to homeless families affected by the hurricane. His name is Jim McIngvale, also known as Mattress Mack. He had approximately 400 people stay in his stores, all while providing three meals a day to everyone.

When Mattress Mack was asked why he did such a kind deed, his response was, "People needed help, and it was the right thing to do."

Mattress Mack didn't sit around waiting to see if anyone else would jump in and help. He didn't sit at his desk and mill around over good intentions. He got up, and he used what he had to make a positive contribution. In my book, this guy is a real life superhero.

Real Life Superheroes:
Practice Generosity, Compassion, and Kindness

"You give not as a debt you owe, but as a seed you sow."

– Oral Roberts

Being generous doesn't always have to boil down to giving dollars. Being generous could mean giving your time, your expertise, or your talent. Maybe if you borrow someone's car, take the time to wash it and gas it up as a way of saying thanks for being so generous. Being generous can be getting someone a gift card for doing a great job. It's paying the toll for the car behind you. It's knowing when your wife gets home after a long day that you have dinner made and the house cleaned. Maybe if you are mowing the yard, and your neighbor's yard looks like it could use a cut, mow it. There are many small, purposeful acts of kindness you can do for others. You can start by just being nice. Look up, smile, and say, "Hi!" It's not hard to do!

Here is a story I ran across that just speaks volumes about the gift of generosity.

Julio Diaz has a daily routine. Every night, the 31-year-old social worker ends his hour-long subway commute to the Bronx one stop early, just so he can eat at his favorite diner.

But one night last month, as Diaz stepped off the No. 6 train and onto a nearly empty platform, his evening took an unexpected turn.

He was walking toward the stairs when a teenage boy approached, and pulled out a knife.

"He wants my money, so I just gave him my wallet and told him, 'Here you go,'" Diaz says.

As the teen began to walk away, Diaz told him, "Hey, wait a minute. You forgot something. If you're going to be robbing people for the rest of the night, you might as well take my coat to keep you warm."

The would-be robber looked at his would-be victim, “like what's going on here?” Diaz says. “He asked me, ‘Why are you doing this?’”

Diaz replied: “If you're willing to risk your freedom for a few dollars, then I guess you must really need the money. I mean, all I wanted to do was get dinner, and if you really want to join me... hey, you're more than welcome.

“You know, I just felt maybe he really needs help,” Diaz says.

Diaz says he and the teen went into the diner and sat in a booth.

“The manager comes by, the dishwashers come by, the waiters come by to say hi,” Diaz says. “The kid was like, ‘You know everybody here. Do you own this place?’”

“No, I just eat here a lot,” Diaz says he told the teen. “He says, ‘But you’re even nice to the dishwasher.’”

Diaz replied, "Well, haven't you been taught you should be nice to everybody?"

"Yea, but I didn't think people actually behaved that way," the teen said.

Diaz asked him what he wanted out of life. "He just had almost a sad face," Diaz says.

The teen couldn't answer Diaz — or he didn't want to.

When the bill arrived, Diaz told the teen, "Look, I guess you're going to have to pay for this bill 'cause you have my money, and I can't pay for this. So, if you give me my wallet back, I'll gladly treat you."

The teen "didn't even think about it," and returned the wallet, Diaz says. "I gave him $20... I figure maybe it'll help him. I don't know."

Diaz says he asked for something in return — the teen's knife — "and he gave it to me."

Afterward, when Diaz told his mother what happened, she said, "You're the type of kid that if someone asked you for the time, you'd give them your watch."

"I figure, you know, if you treat people right, you can only hope that they treat you right. It's as simple as it gets in this complicated world."

Produced for Morning Edition by Michael Garofalo.

There is a little saying, "You may only be someone in the world, but to someone else, you may be the world." A few years ago, I got this amazing story from a friend named Tina. She was standing in line to buy flowers for a ceremony where they honor a "woman of year." The organization is the American Business Woman's Association. As she was waiting, she noticed the gentleman in front of her was growing more impatient with the assistance of the young lady ringing him up. The man grew so impatient that he belted out a reactive comment to the young lady, "What is wrong with you – are you retarded or something?"

The young girl looked at the man, "Yes, sir, I am. Let me get a manager to help assist."

From Tina's standpoint, who works with the Special Olympics, it was evident that the young girl did have Down's Syndrome. When the manager appeared, she assisted the young woman by teaching her how to serve this customer's needs. The young girl apologized to the man for being slow, and wished him a good day. The man never apologized, got what he needed, and walked out.

There were some mixed reviews from the other people waiting in line. Some angry at the guy who said what he did. Others stood there feeling bad for the young girl. Tina was overwhelmed to the point of tears about how the young girl was treated. When she stepped up to get cashed out, the young girl asked, "Are you okay?"

Tina chatted with her, and said, "I think you are doing a great job."

The young girl said, "I just started."

And then she began to praise Tina's flowers.

"Ma'am, these flowers are so beautiful. What are they for?"

"They are a gift for the 'woman of the year.'"

The young girl said, "That is a lucky woman!"

Tina paid the $40 for the beautiful bouquet of flowers, walked around the counter, hugged the young lady, gave her the flowers, and said, "You are the woman of the year to me!"

The young girl started to cry with appreciation.

Tina shared this story on her Facebook wall, and got such overwhelming responses that the local news wanted to do a story about it. Tina refused because she didn't want to make the man who said the unkind words feel worse. In talking with Tina, she hit it right on the head, "My hope is the man understood what he said was not the best choice of words and to learn from it and hopefully become a better person. I didn't want to do the news and have him see that and make him feel worse."

This story is a great example of compassion. To me, compassion is knowing the other person may not be at their best or facing their worst, and you and I are still willing to give the gift of our heart to lift them up.

Real life superheroes practice generosity, compassion, and kindness when the need arises. These qualities are strengths and not weaknesses. Sometimes, we encounter people who reject our kindness or try to take advantage of it, but a superhero discerns what the right thing to do is, and they do it. These special qualities are what truly make a difference because they come from the heart of a real life superhero. They don't just talk about making a difference, they arise and do it.

Real Life Superheroes:

Redirect Rejection and Rudeness to a Better Place

Some people will reject your kindness and generosity. And it's okay. While rejection isn't fun, don't let it steal your joy of giving or acting from a big heart. Don't let it interrupt the nature of who you are. Some people just lack the kind of vision that allows them to see that something special is being done for them. They may even try to take advantage of your kindness, but don't let those villains keep you from being a real life superhero. If they reject you and your gift of kindness, then it is 100% their loss. Some people just won't see your sacrifices, investment of time, thought or heart that goes into the act of kindness or generosity. They miss it! Let it be a lesson that some people will get it, and some people won't.

A good story that highlights this was when my wife was walking by a well-known bakery in downtown Chicago, and she noticed a homeless man sitting outside asking for money as people walked by. My wife, who has a big heart, decided to do something special for the homeless man. She went to the bakery, and bought a cupcake for the homeless man. The cupcake cost almost $10. I remember thinking, Wow, that must be some cupcake. My wife was excited about the prospect of making this person's day with the gift of generosity and a world-famous cupcake.

When she walked outside and handed this amazing cupcake to the homeless man, he gave her a dirty look, and rejected the cupcake by saying, "Don't you know that carbs and sugar can kill you, what are you trying to do to me?!"

It wasn't precisely the response she was planning to hear from him. Instead of recognizing that someone took time out of their day and wallet to help out, his interpretation was negative. Some people might have felt embarrassed and rejected in such a way that trying to demonstrate such kindness in the future was out of the question. However, not my wife. She just thought, Fine, I will find someone who will appreciate this gift. It didn't change her heart from wanting to help. She realized that some people get it, and some people don't. Rejection doesn't have to be a bad thing. You can find the positive in knowing that it will redirect you to a better place.

There was a happy ending to this story. What one homeless man rejected, one 6'6" man accepted. Yep, I got it! That cupcake was so good. If sugar and carbs kill you, I felt like I would have died a happy man because I was in heaven while I was eating that cupcake. Sometimes, the biggest bullies we will encounter are our own thoughts. So, don't let your thoughts belittle you, shrink you, and steal your joy. Evict your defeating thoughts. Invite new ones to bring joy, happiness and life to your thinking.

Superhero Recap

As we approach the end of this book, I want to recap a few important points. I covered this at the start of the book, but I wanted to highlight it one more time, so you can see it again, and recognize the true heart and attitude of a real-life superhero.

RECAP: What Does It Really Mean to Be a Real Life Superhero?

- You don't need a cape or have to be perfect to make a positive difference, just the right heart and a willing attitude.
- You look for the lessons in life's circumstances and grow from them.
- You recognize that adversity is a part of life, but with the right attitude, you can become resilient and keep moving forward.
- You may not have the best of everything, but you make the best of everything you do have.

- You recognize your worth by believing in yourself and creating boundaries from people who don't.
- You have a high appraisal of your attitude, and know it can either work for you or against you.
- You don't always get the credit you deserve, but you give your best, no matter what.
- You lead by example, and believe in creating an environment where people can grow and be productive.
- You would rather encourage people instead of bringing them down.
- You understand that failure is only an event, and not who you are as a person.
- Finally, you are your own unique superhero who was born with purpose. You have the ability every day to make a positive mark in the world. You don't wait for things to happen, you make them happen.

Time to Wrap Things Up

The goal of this book was to expand your mental awareness of how you can be a real life superhero in the important areas of your life. Being a superhero doesn't mean we are perfect every day, but it means we strive toward progress every day to get better, learn, grow, make the most of what we have, persevere through setbacks, believe in our worth, and make a positive mark in the world.

The entire world may not know who you are, but, to someone, you are the world. You are their real life superhero. Because of you, their world is a better place. And that is what it's all about.

As you wrap up this book, keep it close by, and reference it often. It's refreshing and empowering to be reminded of what is important in life, and that our attitude and actions can have a profound impact on others. If you know someone who needs a little boost, lend them your book. You may not get it back, which is my experience. But make it a gift. The best gift a real life superhero can give someone is to help them discover their own personal and professional superpowers, and how they can use those special powers to be a superhero in their world.

Remember, there is a superhero in all of us, ready for action, and looking for opportunities to make a difference. Don't hold your real life superhero back. Life is way too short. Take a deep breath, stand up, and let your superhero out into the real world.

About Sam Glenn, the Attitude Guy

With Sam Glenn, **"It's all about attitude!"** At one time, Sam was one of the most negative people you could ever meet. However, something changed – Sam's way of thinking. When you change your thinking, you change everything! As a result, Sam found a new path for his life and a way to bring value to others through his inspirational books, art and speeches.

Sam never set out to be a motivational speaker or an author. He started by teaching Sunday school and eventually his audiences grew to 75,000 people at stadium events. For the past twenty years, Sam Glenn has become widely known in the meeting and events industry as one of the most entertaining and energizing speakers at Sam has won several national awards for his motivational training videos and empowering speeches on ATTITUDE. Sam and his family currently reside in Carmel, Indiana, but are originally from Minnesota. Sam's growing speaking business has become what it is today because of super fans and word of mouth. Sam loves to connect with his fans at events and on social media.

If you would like to learn more about how to book Sam Glenn to speak at your next meeting, in-service, training event or conference, visit Sam's speaking website: **(www.SamGlenn.com)**

•••

To Inquire about Sam Speaking at

Your Next Event or Conference,

Email Sam's office:

Imfo@SamGlenn.com

•••

Visit the Official Website for

Sam Glenn:

www.SamGlenn.com

•••

Made in the USA
Las Vegas, NV
12 September 2024

95133156R00075